THE MYSTERY OF PSALM 91

Under the Shadow of the Almighty, God's Promises and Prayers for Protection

TAIWO OLUKOYEDE

Table of Contents

INTRODUCTION

For several years, the world as we know it has been turned upside down by a series of events that are not in the positive and do not appeal to our sense of peace and justice. Extremism, terrorism, gunviolence, drugs, the COVID-19 pandemic, human and sex trafficking, organ harvesting and other national and international misfortunes made the world a more dangerous place.

Several people lost access to their source of livelihood during the national lockdown caused by the COVID-19 pandemic while some people lost it to cyber-crimes. Some lost countless properties, some have lost loved ones in various attacks and many others have lost their entire villages or towns to attacks and raids carried out on their communities during different Boko Haram or banditry raids. Therefore, many people committed suicide because of their losses. Due to this monumental disaster in history, it's hard not to be anxious or worry and one doesn't have to look too far before Psalm 91 shows up on their newsfeed. This is so for no other reason than the fact that Psalm 91 is the 9-1-1 emergency code these days to our mighty God (Riggleman, 2020).

So why are millions of Christians around the world praying Psalm 91? This is so simply because it has become our emergency number in these trying times. It assures us of God's protection in times of trouble. The power of Psalm is a reminder that no matter what happens, a financial collapse, job loss, war, terminal diseases, epidemics, pandemics or even attacks, God is still in control. In the very first two verses, we are told exactly who God is.

The psalm begins with the beautiful verses:

> *"Whoever dwells in the shelter of the Most High will rest in the shadow of the Almighty." Psalm 91:1*

> *"I will say of the LORD, "He is my refuge and my fortress, my God, in whom I trust." Psalm 91:2*

This book can't be timelier than now. We shall take a look into the mystery of this age long and powerful Psalm. Read it prayerfully and you will see you and your family enjoy increased divine protection.

CHAPTER ONE
Background Of Psalm 91

Psalm 91 is very powerful and unique in many different ways. Until today, the author of the Psalm is unknown. Although many Bible scholars think it is Moses who authored it, because it shares some similarities with Psalm 27 and 31, some other scholars attribute the Psalm to King David. Frank Derek Kidner, a British Old Testament scholar, best known for writing commentaries holds this belief about Psalm 91:

"Some of its language, of strongholds and shields, reminds us of David, to whom the Septuagint ascribes it; other phrases echo the Song of Moses in Deuteronomy 32, as did Psalm 90; but it is in fact, anonymous and timeless, perhaps all the more accessible for that." (Kidner, 1975)

Countless other notable Bible scholars have described Psalm 91 in wonderful ways. Among them is Reverend Doctor George Campbell Morgan (D.D.), a British evangelist, preacher, leading Bible teacher, and a prolific author, who preached his first sermon at 13. He noted the wonderful character of this psalm: "This psalm is one of the greatest possessions of the saints." (Morgan, 1978)

Spurgeon opines about Psalm 91: "In the whole collection there is not a more cheering Psalm, its tone is elevated and sustained throughout, faith is at its best, and speaks nobly." (Spurgeon, 2011)

Simeon de Muis, a French churchman and Hebraist, professor at the Collège du roi from 1614, and biblical commentator, continues on Psalm 91:

It is one of the most excellent works of this kind which has ever appeared. It is impossible to imagine anything more solid, more beautiful, more profound, or more ornamented (Spurgeon, 2011).

From a reader's perspective, this psalm is a popular favorite of many Christians. Reading it at any time reminds me of myself as a little boy, standing before cathedral pews and reading it out as recitations. The imagery of hiding under a big covering to avoid evil or an attack always came alive whenever I read it then. Even as an adult, it turns out to be my favorite Psalm in the Bible. Similarly, it is many people's favorite, as it turns out.

I think the Psalm is a popular favorite because of its powerful theme of divine protection, especially in a world that is filled with so much evil. Psalm 91 is quoted as being one of – if not the – most powerful chapters and prayers of the entire Holy Bible in this regard. Most times, it is invoked during times of danger, uncertainty, and evil attacks. When we pray with and believe in the words of Psalm 91, truly trusting in the Lord, we need not fear the power and deception of the enemy. This makes this Psalm very unique. We bring before God His promises of protection and safety whenever we pray Psalm 91.

In Jewish thought, Psalm 91 conveys the ideas of God's protection and rescue from danger (Morrison, 2017). Often in times past, the Psalm was considered a "song of evil spirits" or "plagues" in Jewish communities. The idea was that it has the power to protect from plagues or evil spirits when recited in prayer. For example, in the time of the Geonim (the presidents of the two great Babylonian Talmudic Academies of Sura and Pumbedita, in the Abbasid Caliphate, who were the generally accepted spiritual leaders of the Jewish community worldwide in the early medieval era), Psalm 91 was recited to drive away demons (Matt, 2004). Most of them believed that at the recitation of the Psalm, demons would flee. Similarly, Psalm 91 was added as one of the "Four Psalms Against Demons" in the Dead Sea Scroll because of its protection and deliverance theme (VanderKam, 2005). Modern-day Christians see the psalm as a source of comfort and protection, even in times of suffering (Deffinbaugh, 2004).

Whenever you need the Lord's protection over your life and that of your family, pray and meditate on Psalm 91. When you prayerfully and slowly read over this psalm, you unlock God's power of protection and preservation over you and your family. It is recommended that you meditate on it daily. Reflect on what God is promising you specifically. Don't wait until you have a specific danger before you pray with Psalm 91. If possible, memorize your favorite verse(s) and repeat them often throughout the day. Then in times of great danger, need and uncertainty, if committed to memory, the Holy Spirit will graciously remind you of what God has promised you. These words will reassure you of God's protection, those you love, and the whole world around you.

Having seen a bit about its background, let us take a look at the whole Psalm 91, and afterward take a deep look into the verses.

Psalm 91

¹ *Whoever dwells in the shelter of the Most High will rest in the shadow of the Almighty.*

[2] I will say of the LORD, "He is my refuge and my fortress, my God, in whom I trust." [3] Surely, he will save you

from the fowler's snare and from the deadly pestilence. [4] He will cover you with his feathers, and under his wings you will find refuge; his faithfulness will be your shield and rampart.

[5] You will not fear the terror of night, nor the arrow that flies by day,

[6] nor the pestilence that stalks in the darkness, nor the plague that destroys at midday. [7] A thousand may fall at your side, ten thousand at your right hand, but it will not come near you. [8] You will only observe with your eyes and see the punishment of the wicked.

[9] If you say, "The LORD is my refuge," and you make the Most High your dwelling,

10   no harm will overtake you, no
disaster will come near your tent.

11   For he will command his angels
concerning you

to guard you in all your ways; 12

they will lift you up in their hands,

so that you will not strike your

foot against a stone.

13 You will tread on the lion and the cobra;
you will trample the great lion and the
serpent.

14 "Because he[b] loves me," says the LORD, "I
will rescue him;

I will protect him, for he acknowledges my
name.

15 He will call on me, and I will answer him;

I will be with him in trouble, I

will deliver him and honor

him. 16 With long life I will

satisfy him and show him my

salvation."

Say this Prayer

Heavenly Father, I Thank You for Your continued presence with me and my family. I Thank You for Your Almighty wings which cast an impenetrable shadow of protection. Thank You for going before me; and for covering us from behind. Thank You for choosing to be in me through your Holy Spirit, and for lifting my burdens. Cover me in your secret place now and forevermore, in the Mighty Name of Jesus I pray, Amen.

CHAPTER TWO
Meaning In Verses

Psalm 91 begins with the strong statement that God is our refuge, our fortress, and our place of safety (verses 1-4).

Whoever dwells in the shelter of the Most High

will rest in the shadow of the Almighty.

I will say of the LORD, "He is my refuge and my fortress,   my God, in whom I trust." 3 Surely, he will save you   from the fowler's snare

and from the deadly pestilence.

> [4] *He will cover you with his feathers,*
> *and under his wings you will find refuge;*
> *his faithfulness will be your shield and*
> *rampart.*

Everyone loves to read Psalms 91, but it starts with a powerful statement that describes whom this psalm applies to. If you want to enjoy God's protection like it was described in Psalms 91, then you must understand the deeper meaning of this powerful chapter! Its theme speaks of God's almighty power in protecting us regardless of what the situation may be. Generally, it begins by describing two sets of people:

- *The Delivered*
- *The Destroyed*

The first group of those who God will deliver are those who fear Him. It is a seal of a promise to protect them through thick and thin. The other group is those that are wide open to destruction. This reveals to us that the earth is at the mercy of sin and its effects of death and destruction. Those who will escape destruction are those who have Almighty God as their trust and confidence. The two groups of people have two different destinies. God is only committed to protecting those who have accepted and trusted Him. the other group is open to Satan's wild destruction. The Bible text in 1 Peter 5:8 paints a clearer picture:

> *Be sober, be vigilant, because your adversary the devil walketh about as a roaring lion, seeking whom he may devour. –*

1 Peter 5:8

The destiny of those who do not know God or surrender to His sovereignty is open to be devoured by the devil and his cohorts. This is simply a result of a sin-infested world. This is why we find comfort in Psalm 91. Not because it promises a long, trouble-free life on this present earth, but because it assures us that in Christ, we would escape the wrath of God. In this life, we do not need to fear any danger or even death, for God is even capable to raise us from death to eternal life, in His presence when he comes again. This is our hope. This hope is not for everyone, but only for those who have turned to God for their security and safety. Jesus Christ suffered the wrath of God, and by faith in Him, we may be sheltered from it. Sharing in this hope requires that you must trust in the Savior, the Lord Jesus Christ. May you and your family experience the safety and protection of God, in Christ's name.

What does the 'secret place' of Psalm 91 mean?

There are many different meanings alluded to in the concept of the secret place in the first verse of Psalm 91. For the theologians who believe that Moses wrote the Psalm, the 'secret place' may have its reference to "Goshen" where the children of Israel lived throughout the plagues in Egypt and never suffered like the Egyptians. Goshen was a place of divine protection for the Israelites in the same land of Egypt, where Pharaoh and his people suffered God's wrath. To some of those Bible scholars who believe the Psalm was written by King David, the secret place could represent the places where David hid from his numerous escapades with his enemies.

However, the "secret place" in Psalm 91 refers generally to the Lord's shelter. The "shelter" being referred to in the first verse is (actually) a 'fortress' or a 'tower.' The Jerusalem Bible states as follows:

> *"If you live in the shelter of Elyon (High), and make your home in the shadow of Shaddai (God), you can say to Yahweh: My refuge, my fortress, my God in whom I trust!" Amen.*

It is therefore imperative to always answer the question, "Who will God protect?" Psalms 91 starts with the statement, "He who dwells in the secret place of the Most High." With this statement,

Psalms 91 makes it clear right from the start whom God will protect.

God protects His own. He will protect those who choose to live for Him and act upon that decision.

While it is true that God can protect anyone whom He wishes, those who constantly live a life close to God will receive special treatment. They can live in peace, serenity, and security because of God's assurance that they will be protected.

Now, notice, the text says, "He who dwells." It didn't say, "He who dwelt" or "He who will dwell." It is in the present tense. God won't protect those who stopped dwelling with Him or those who didn't make the decision yet to be with Him. It means that the one whom God will protect is someone who actively lives a life that glorifies Him.

The word "dwells" came from the Hebrew word *yashab*, which means to "sit down, settle, remain, and inhabit." As you can see, dwelling in God's presence is a conscious choice. It is something that we decide to do, not out of necessity or grudge, but out of a willing heart.

Dwelling in the secret place of the Most High means that we constantly seek His love, comfort, and protection. God will protect those who want to know Him better and on a deeper level. Compare that to those people who don't live a godly life.

They expose their lives to many dangers and unnecessary pain and suffering. You must make sure that you are dwelling in the secret place of the Most High every day. This is the only guarantee of protection from the whirls of the devil and his agents.

This secret place is ruled over by the Almighty God. Therefore, God's secret place is the safest location in the universe. Therefore, you must ensure that you are walking in righteousness. God's covering is all over everyone who fears him. these are the ones that God is committed to watching over.

> *The eyes of the LORD are on the righteous, and his ears are attentive to their cry –*

Psalm 34:15

Imagine a huge umbrella shade under which people would run to when the sunlight is scorching or it is raining. Now you have a clue about what the secret place of the Almighty means. The all-powerful God will shield all those who dwell with him. They shall remain under his care as guests under the protection of their host.

In the Old Sanctuary system of sin cleansing, according to God's instructions to Moses, in the Most Holy Place, the wings of the cherubim were the most conspicuous objects, and they probably suggested to the psalmist the expression used here. To King David, it would symbolize the mountains and caves where he hid while he fled from King Saul. The secret place of the Almighty God would mean to us the promises of God and the demonstration of his power of deliverance and protection as we find in the scriptures. When we hold these promises firm in faith so much so that they become palpable to us, fear of destruction flees from us.

Those who commune with God in fellowship are safe with Him, no evil can reach them, for the outstretched wings of his power and love cover them from all harm. This protection is constant – they abide under it, and it is all-sufficient, for it is the shadow of the Almighty, whose omnipotence will surely screen them from all attack. What a mighty shadow!

Many followers of Jesus Christ seem to know very little of the secret place of the Most High or what it is to abide under His shadow. This is truly the bane of many Christians – lost to open destruction when they have access to absolute protection. Many seem to regard this as only a thing for pastors or super-spiritual brethren. Think about King David for a minute like he wrote this Psalm. He was a spot-on warrior and man well acquainted with the realities of life. The life of the spirit indeed seems to come more easily for some than for others, but there is an aspect of the secret place of the Most High that is for everyone who puts his trust in Him. As Spurgeon fires,

> *"Every child of God looks towards the inner sanctuary and the mercy-seat, yet all do not dwell in the most holy place; they run to it at times, and enjoy occasional approaches, but they do not habitually reside in the mysterious*

presence" (Spurgeon, 2011)

Comparing the 'secret place' and 'The shadow of the Almighty we must understand that the latter implies great nearness. We must walk very close to a companion if we would have his shadow fall on us. This means that we have a responsibility to activating the shadow of God's protection. We must develop a relationship with God through the Holy Spirit that makes us dwell under his shadow. When we willfully stray away from God, we can't expect His shadow to cover us because you have to be close to someone to have their shadow cover you.

Spurgeon, while explaining the poetry of Frances Ridley Havergal suggested four ways the Scripture speaks of the shadow of the Almighty:

- *The shadow of the rock (Isaiah 32:2).*

- *The shadow of the tree (Song of Solomon 2:3)*

- *The shadow of His wings (Psalm 63:7).*

- *The shadow of His hand (Isaiah 49:2)* (Havergal, 1881).

So much for God's shadow of protection. Here are a few things to reflect upon:

- *Are you striving to dwell in God's secret place?*
- *Are you constantly looking for ways to stay close to God?*

- *Do you have that yearning to be on God's side every single moment of your life?*

I hope your answer to these questions is yes and if not, then change the way you live. God is eager and is more than willing to take care of you. All you have to do is stay in God's secret place and be at peace with Him.

CHAPTER THREE
The Names of God

In this chapter, we shall take a deeper look at the essence of Psalm 91, unveiling more sacred truths in its verses. Although the previous chapter has explained the first four verses, we shall dig a little deeper in finding the mystery of the names of God as used by the author of Psalm 91.

At a closer reading, we observe that Verse 1 opens with the ancient names for God "Most High" (ElElyon) and "Almighty" (Shaddai). El-Elyon repeats in verse 9, as well as YHWH, the proper name of the God of Israel, making these names synonyms for one another. This happens again in verse 9.

Succinctly, these first two verses of Psalm 91 use four wonderful titles or names for God:

Most High God: El-Elyon –

In Hebrew, it is rendered as אֵל עֶלְיוֹן. This name of God was used first in Genesis to describe the God of Melchizedek, the King of Salem. El-Elyon is a poetic synonym of Yahweh (Della, 1944). The name acknowledges God as the Highest of all gods that are known and unknown. Simply put, it is translated as "Most High God". When you consider this in the context of Psalm 91, it describes the kind of Supreme being under whose shadow protection is guaranteed.

When we describe God as the Most High, we agree that there can be nothing higher than Him no matter how ho high they seem. When Abraham paid tithes to Melchizedek (Gen 14:17-22) this is the name by which the priest worshiped God. This priest, "resembling the Son of God," said to

Abraham,

> *"Blessed be Abram by God Most*
> *High, maker of heaven and earth;*
> *And blessed be God Most High,*

> *who has delivered your enemies into your hand!"* –

Genesis 14:19

In an interesting story in 1 Samuel 5:1-8, we are helped to understand the meaning of the Most High God being referred to in Psalm 91. After the Philistines had captured the Ark of the Covenant, they set it beside their idol, Dagon. The next day, Dagon fell over bowing before the Most High God. The Philistines set their idol back up, and the next day, Dagon fell again, this time breaking its head and hands. The Most High God in this story is proving there is no idol or anything that can stand beside or above Him. This is the same God spoken of here in Psalm 91, inviting us to dwell in His secret place.

The Most High invites you to know Him more personally today. To know Him, you must recognize He exists (Hebrews 11:6). Then you must acknowledge Him concerning everything (Exodus

20:3; Isaiah 46:9-11). You can never dwell in His secret place while trying to place yourself in the secret place of other false gods in your life.

Almighty: Shaddai

Amy Grant's song in 1982 made the name "El Shaddai" famous. Although the song was written by Michael Card and John Thompson for Card's 1981 debut album, the powerful song is more closely associated with Grant. As she sang, "Age to age you're still the same, by the power of the name," she magnified God Almighty–the wonderful "El Shaddai." This song made the name El Shaddai very popular even today.

Psalm 91 speaks of abiding under the shadow of El-
Shaddai – the Almighty God. In Hebrew, it is written as שַׁדַּי אל. The first occurrence of the name is in Genesis 17:1:

> *"When Abram was ninety-nine years old the Lord appeared to Abram and said to him, 'I am El Shaddai; walk*

before me, and be blameless" (ESV)

Similarly, in Genesis 35:11 God says to Jacob, "I am El Shaddai: be fruitful and multiply; a nation and a company of nations shall be of thee, and kings shall come out of thy loins" (ESV). According to Exodus 6:2-3, Shaddai was the name by which God was known to Abraham, Isaac, and Jacob. We find the name again in the Book of Job.

> *"And the Lord said to Job: 'Shall a faultfinder contend with the Almighty? He who argues with God, let him answer it'" –*

Job 40:1–2

A better foundational meaning of El Shaddai may be the phrase, *"The Overpowerer,"* which emphasizes God's power to achieve all His purposes (Exodus 15:6; Matthew 19:26). Qualifying His power in this way is important, as the Bible never suggests God can do everything and anything. God's strength is perfect and cannot be increased or diminished (Sproul, 2020).

Ultimately, no one or anything can keep Him from accomplishing His sovereign decrees (Psalms 115:3). Therefore, when we speak of the shadow of the Almighty God as portrayed in Psalm 91, we understand that it means being protected from all forms of evil and destruction.

When we consider the experience of Job and his struggles to understanding the complexity of El Shaddai, we find the word El Shaddai in the Book of Job more than any other book of the Bible. God gives Job a particularly clear and breathtaking description and demonstration of His power (Job 38–42). Job spends most of the book questioning God's purposes, but the Lord's display of His wisdom and power finally silences him.

> *"Then Job answered the Lord: 'I am unworthy—how can I reply to you? I put my hand over my mouth. I spoke once, but I have no answer— twice, but I will say no more'"* – **Job 40:3–5**

The same would be our answer - silence – at an Almighty God. We get under his shadow by drawing closer to Him through our relationship with the Holy Ghost.

The Lord: Yahweh

"*I will say of the LORD, He is my refuge and my fortress...*" – **Psalm 91:2a**. Another name of God that appears in the second verse of Psalm 91 is Yahweh.

Exodus 3:13-15 is the first Biblical usage of the name "Yahweh," and we can see at the end of the passage that it is the name by which God has chosen to be remembered throughout all generations. This divine name of God was increasingly regarded as too sacred to be uttered; it was thus replaced vocally in the synagogue ritual by the Hebrew word Adonai ("My Lord").

The English language doesn't have an exact translation of the word "Yahweh," so in our Old Testament we see it written as "LORD" in all capital letters. The name, Yahweh (yah-WEH) occurs more than 6,800 times in the Old

Testament (Martin, 2019). It appears in every book but Esther, Ecclesiastes, and the Song of Songs. As the sacred, personal name of Israel's God, it was eventually spoken aloud only by priests worshiping in the Jerusalem temple.

English editions of the Bible usually translate Adonai as "Lord" and Yahweh as "LORD." Yahweh is the name that is most closely linked to God's redeeming acts in the history of his chosen people. We know God because of what he has done. In Psalm 91, this name of God is used to describe the personal relationship that the author expects us to have with God: "I will say of the LORD…" It doesn't say, "They will say of the LORD" or "I heard them say of the LORD". It is personal in its declaration.

God will never end. If he did not come into being he cannot go out of being, because he is being. The name Yahweh means that God is the absolute reality. There is no reality before Him or that will come outside Him. Yahweh doesn't need any approval whatsoever to do whatever He pleases. He does whatever he deems right, and because

He has done it, it is absolutely right. So, when the Psalmist says, "I will say of the Yahweh...He is my refuge..." (Psalm 91:2), he is making declarations based on these realities of the meaning of Yahweh! When you declare it like the Psalmist in Psalm 91, you are simply telling all of creation, including

Satan and his buddies to listen to what the Sovereign God says concerning your safety and protection.

My God: Elohay

Elohim, singular **Elohay**, (Hebrew: God), is the God of Israel in the Old Testament (Britannica, 1998). It is the first name for God found in the Bible, and it's used throughout the Old Testament over 2,300 times. Elohim comes from the Hebrew root meaning "strength" or "power" and has the unusual characteristic of being plural in form.

In Genesis 1:1, we read, "In the beginning, Elohim created the heaven and the earth." Right from the start, this plural form for the name of God is used to describe the One God, a mystery that is uncovered throughout the rest of the Bible. Throughout scripture, all the way to Psalm 91, Elohim is used to personalize God, the creator. When we pray like the Psalmist, "My God" we are declaring his power to create all things. We declare that He is the God of the Beginning. This is particularly interesting when we see the way it is personalized: "My God of the Beginning!"

To be able to personalize God in this way in Psalm 91 requires intimacy. We must give ourselves completely to God. He must have our attention. He is before all things in time and priority. He must be the first above all our affections and that way He will be your shelter.

In the contemporary world, we live in today, many things require our attention and devotion – our jobs, our children, our spouses, our hobbies, our phones, our hobbies, our businesses, and the list never ends. The demands and distractions of life in inundating outrageous.

We, therefore, have to be careful not to let them become more important or give them more priority than our relationship with God. How many of the things that occupy our time, money, hobbies, and attention have taken the place that belongs to God? Anything can become a god to us; anything we put an excessive amount of time on. Even our feelings can become a god if we let them control us. The key to having the "abundant life" of God, His protection, His safety, His love, peace, and joy, is keeping him in the number one place in our priorities always.

CHAPTER FOUR
My Refuge

I will say of the LORD, He is my refuge and my fortress: my God; in him will I trust.

Psalm 91:2

The Merriam-Webster Dictionary describes a refuge as:

- *shelter or protection from danger or distress*
- *a place that provides shelter or protection*
- *something to which one has recourse in difficulty*

It is from this root word that the word, refugee takes its root. A refugee is someone distressed or in trouble. Refugees receive refuge in refugee camps. A common example is victims of war, religious, or political persecution. When lifethreatening situations arise, refugees seek a place of refuge. For example, David was being pursued by King Saul to kill him. King Saul killed an entire community because they gave David refuge. David ran from cave to cave, hiding from Saul for at least over 10 good years!

Now Verse 2 pf Psalm 91 in Hebrew a first-person declaration of trust in YHWH: "I will say" – that God is my refuge (which repeats in v4 and 9) and fortress – a defensive position, sometimes translated "stronghold" or "castle." Then, the psalm switches to "you" – and reads as a consequence of this declaration.

Verses 3-6 blend and develop three different images of protection: the image of the bird, the image of a warrior, and something else. The reference to the fowler; a hunter who stalks and catches birds specifically, the pinions, which are technically wings rather than legs, and the wings all position the reader as a nestling under the protection of its parent.

I will say of the LORD, He is my refuge and my fortress: my God; in him will I trust. Surely, he shall deliver thee from the snare of the fowler, and from the noisome pestilence. He shall cover thee with his feathers, and under his wings shalt thou trust: his truth shall be thy shield and buckler. Thou shalt not be afraid for the terror by night; nor for the arrow that flieth by day – **Psalm 91:2-5**

The shield and buckler are presumably some kinds of military equipment. We can describe it as a special type of shield that surrounded the person on four sides. The references to pestilence (verse 3 and 6), terror (verse 5), and destruction (verse 6) are all, references to the demons' evil activities of Satan. A lot of things can be pestilential, as we know. Whatever their origin, demonic or natural, these things to fear are there night and day, in the depths of darkness and the glare of noonday. In other words, all the time.

Surely, he shall deliver thee from the snare of the fowler. Assuredly no subtle plot shall succeed against one who has the eyes of God watching for his defense, We are foolish and weak as poor little birds and are very apt to be lured to our destruction by cunning foes, but if we dwell near to God, he will see to it that the most skillful deceiver shall not entrap us.

He who is a Spirit can protect us from evil spirits, he who is mysterious can rescue us from mysterious dangers, he who is immortal can redeem himself from mortal sickness. There is a deadly pestilence of error like the corvid19 pandemic; we are safe from that if we dwell in communion with the God of truth. There is a fatal pestilence of sin, we shall not be infected by it if we abide with the thrice Holy One. Also, there is a pestilence of disease, and even from that calamity, our faith shall win immunity if it is of that high order which abides in God, walks on in calm serenity, and ventures all things for duty's sake.

Everyone seems to read the thousands and ten thousand in verse 7 as the wicked in verse 8. In other words, the "you" being addressed here is surrounded and seriously outnumbered by the wicked. The only way of surviving here is because one is dwelling in God's secret place and the shadow of the Almighty. This is only how you don't get to fear a thousand and ten thousand wicked forces at your right and left. You will not fear because God is your refuge.

In the fourth verse, it declares:

"He shall cover thee with thy feathers, and under his wings shalt thou trust."

A wonderful expression! We can only admire and adore such a level of protection symbolized here. Does the Lord speak of his feathers, as though he likened himself to a bird? Who will not see herein a matchless love, a divine tenderness, which should both woo and win our confidence?

The Almighty God covers us like a hen covers its chickens from the preying mandate of the hawks. He protects our souls in like manner for comfort and safety. Hawks in the sky and snares in the field are equally harmless when we nestle so near the Lord. His truth --his true promise, and his faithfulness to his promise, shall be thy shield and buckler. We have Double armor when we rely on God's protection.

Furthermore, picture the Almighty God bearing a shield and wearing an all-surrounding coat of mail.

God will quench all fiery darts fired by the devil against us when we dwell in His shelter.

Verse 8 states:

"Only with thine eyes shalt thou behold and see the reward of the wicked."

What a sight this must be! The sight reveals both the justice and the mercy of God; in them, that perish the severity of God will be manifest, and in the believer's escape the richness of divine goodness will be apparent. Joshua and Caleb verified this promise. The sight of God's judgments softens the heart, excites solemn awe, creates gratitude, and so stirs up the deepest kind of adoration. It is such a sight as none of us would wish to see, and yet if we did see it, we might thus be lifted to the very noblest style of manhood. One case may not be judged alone lest we misjudge, but instances of divine visitation will be plentiful in the memory of any attentive observer of men and things; from all these put together we may fairly draw conclusions, and unless we shut our eyes to that which is self-evident, we shall soon perceive that there is, after all, a moral ruler over the sons of men, who sooner or later rewards the ungodly with due punishment.

Verses 11-13 are famous enough that Satan quotes them at Jesus in Matthew 4 and Luke 4. Speaking of Jesus, Christian readers may want to let what we know about Jesus' story inform our understanding of these verses. They do not signify that the one who dwells in the shelter of the Most High will never experience crucifixion. Jesus' response to Satan in the wilderness may even suggest that.

God's first-person, direct, unambiguous promises in verses 14-16 are, similarly, not promises of trouble-free experience, but God's presence in trouble, and of ultimate rescue, honor, and salvation. Long life (verse 16), literally "length of days" or "long days," is one of the explicit promises. If trouble is a battle we are in the thick of, this promise is encouraging – in much the same way.

CHAPTER FIVE
God's Promises In Psalm 91

Psalm 91 is a great truth laid down in general for all of us who trust God and develop a relationship with Him. All those who live a life of communion with God are constantly safe under his protection, and may therefore preserve a holy serenity and security of mind at all times:

"He that dwells, that sits down, in the secret place of the Most High, shall abide under the shadow of the Almighty" – **Psalm 91:1**

In other words, he that by faith chooses God as his guardian shall find all full package in him, which he needs or can desire. It is the character of a true believer that he dwells in the secret place of the Most High; he is at home in God, returns to God, and reposes in him as his rest; he acquaints himself with inward religion, and makes heart-work of the service of God, worships within the veil, and loves to be alone with God, to converse with him in solitude.

This is just the privilege and comfort of those that do so that they abide under the shadow of the Almighty. He shelters them and comes between them and everything that would annoy them, whether storm or sunshine. They shall not only have an admittance but a residence, under God's protection; he will be their rest and refuge forever.

As we see in the second verse, the psalmist comfortably applies this to himself: "I will say of the Lord, whatever others say of him, "He is my refuge; I choose him as such and confide in him. Others make idols their refuge, but I will say of Jehovah, the true and living God, He is my refuge: any other is a refuge of lies. He is a refuge that will not fail me; for he is my fortress and strong-hold."

Idolaters called their idols Mahuzzim, their most strong-hold (Dan. 11:39), but therein they deceived themselves. Only those who secure themselves in God and that make the LORD their God, will he be their fortress. There is no reason to question God's sufficiency. If Jehovah is our God, our refuge, and our fortress, what can we desire which we may not be sure to find in him? He is neither fickle nor false, neither weak nor mortal; he is God and not man, and therefore there is no danger of being disappointed in him. We know whom we have trusted.

The psalmist assures believers of divine protection, from his own experience; and that which he says is the word of God, and what we may rely upon.

That, whatever happens to them, nothing shall hurt them (v. 10)

There shall no evil befall thee; though trouble or affliction befall thee, yet there shall be no real evil in it, for it shall come from the love of God and shall be sanctified; it shall come, not for thy hurt, but thy good; and though, for the present, it is not joyous but grievous, yet, in the end, it shall yield so well that thou thyself shalt own no evil befall thee. It is not an evil, an only evil, but there is a mixture of good in it and a product of good by it. By your dwelling, you shall be taken under the divine protection: There shall no plague come nigh that, nothing and no one will do you any damage.

That the angels of light shall be serviceable to them, (verses 11, 12).

This is a precious promise and speaks a great deal both of honor and comfort to the saints. According to Psalm 91, the angels have been charge concerning different aspects:

The charge is to keep thee in all thy ways –

This is isn't a promise to the church of God in general. This is a personal charge that God has given to His angels to keep you in all His ways. Therefore, those that go out of that way put themselves out of God's protection. When Satan quoted this scripture while tempting Jesus Christ, he left out this later part because he intends to distort the truth. The angels of God are committed to keeping us in the ways that are honorable to God. When you examine the extent of the promise; it is to keep thee in all thy ways: even where there is no apparent danger yet we need it, and where there is the most imminent danger, we shall have it. Wherever the saints go the angels are charged with them, as the servants are with the children. The charge is given to the angels concerning the saints. He who is the Lord of the angels, who gave them their being and gives laws to them, whose they are and whom they were made to serve, he shall give his angels a charge over thee, not only over the church in general but over every particular believer. The angels keep the charge of the Lord their God, and this is the charge they receive from him. It denotes the great care God takes of the saints, in that the angels themselves shall be charged with them, and employed for them.

The angels of God shall bear thee up in their hands –

which denotes both their great ability and their great affection. They can bear up the saints out of the reach of danger, and they do it with all the tenderness and affection wherewith the nurse carries the little child about in her arms. This speaks of how helpless we are, and how helpful the angels are unto us. They are dutiful in their ministrations by keeping the feet of the saints, lest they dash them against a stone, lest they stumble and fall into sin and trouble.

That the powers of darkness shall be triumphed over by the angels of God for you (verse 13)

"Thou shalt tread upon the lion and adder…" is the kind of assurance of protection against evil that the promise seals for us. Halleluyah! The devil is called a roaring lion, the old serpent, the red dragon; so that to this promise the apostle seems to refer in that (Rom. 16:20). The God of peace shall tread Satan under your feet. Christ has broken the serpent's head, spoiled our spiritual enemies (Col. 2:15).

Through Christ, we are more than conquerors. Like Joshua commanded Christ calls us like the captains of Israel, to come and set our feet on the necks of vanquished enemies. Surely, this promise has transcended Psalm 91 and extends into the full accomplishment in Christ, and the miraculous power which he had over the whole creation – healing the sick, casting out devils, and particularly putting it into his disciples' commission that they should take up serpents

They shall take up serpents; and if they drink any deadly thing, it shall not hurt them; they shall lay hands on the sick, and they shall recover. – **Mark 16:18**

This promise is so powerful. It can also be applied to that care of the divine providence by which we are preserved from ravenous poisonous creatures. The wild beasts of the field shall be at peace with you (Job 5:23).

God will, in due time, deliver us out of trouble

"I will deliver him" (verse 14 and again verse 15) is God's towering promise. This promise designates a double deliverance – living and dying. This simply means deliverance in trouble and deliverance out of trouble. It doesn't matter if you have entered into trouble or out of trouble, the Almighty LORD has promised to deliver you.

God will, in the meantime, be with you in trouble (verses 15) –

If God does not immediately put a period to afflictions, yet they shall have his gracious presence with them in their troubles. The Almighty God will take notice of your sorrows, and know your soul in adversity. He has promised to visit you graciously by his Word and Spirit. He will converse with you and support and comfort you. God's promise is the surest token of His presence in all our troubles.

God has promised to answer our prayers

"He shall call upon me; He shall call upon me, and I will answer him..." (Verse 15).

Furthermore, in Psalm 58, the Psalmist exclaims of God, "I will pour upon him the spirit of prayer, and then I will answer (Psalms 85:8). God's answer to our prayers is premised upon His promise. He answers us by providence and mercy, bringing in seasonal relief to our troubles as we call upon

Him. God answers us by His grace and extending to us such grace to strengthen us in our souls (Psalms 138:3). He showed unto Apostle Paul such a similar grace, with grace sufficient to overcome his earthly challenges (2 Co. 12:9).

God will exalt and dignify us:

"I will set him on high," (verse 14) means that God will take us out of the reach of trouble; above the stormy region, on a rock above the waves.

He shall dwell on high: his place of defense shall be the munitions of rocks: bread shall be given him; his waters shall be sure. – **Isaiah 33:16**

They shall be enabled, by the grace of God, to look down upon the things of this world with a holy contempt and indifference. This is the ability to look up to the things of the other world with a holy ambition and concern, and then they are set on high. "I will honor him" refers to those who are truly honorable, whom God puts honor upon by taking them into covenant and communion with himself and designing them for his kingdom and glory

If any man serve me, let him follow me; and where I am, there shall also my servant be: if any man serve me, him will my Father honour. – **John 12:26**

We shall have a sufficiency of life in this world (verse 16)

"With length of days will I satisfy him..."

This promise means that:

- **We shall live long enough**: We shall be in this world till we have done the work we were sent into this world for and are ready for heaven, and that is long enough.

- **We shall be satisfied enough**: God by his grace shall wean us from the world and make us willing to leave it when we have fulfilled our days. This means we shall be satisfied with the number of our days and the quality of life.

We shall have eternal life in the other world –

This crowns the blessedness: "I will show him my salvation" (verse 16)! God has promised us sure salvation not just from the troubles of this world, but also the word itself. The is the eternal life that Jesus came to deliver unto us in the world.

> *For God so loved the world, that he gave his only begotten Son, that whosoever believeth in him should not perish, but have everlasting life. –*

John 3:16

God has shown us the Messiah. When the good old Simeon saw Jesus in the temple being dedicated, he was then satisfied with long life when he could say, "For mine eyes have seen thy salvation, Which thou hast prepared before the face of all people; A light to lighten the Gentiles, and the glory of thy people Israel" (Luke 2:30-32).

There is no greater joy to the Old-Testament saints than to see Christ's day, though at a distance. It is more probably that the word refers to the better country, that is, the heavenly, which the patriarchs desired and sought (Hebrews 11. Although we see through a glass darkly, in the meantime, God will give us a prospect of it. All these promises in Psalm 91 ultimately point primarily to Christ and had their accomplishment in his resurrection and exaltation.

Who is Eligible for these Promises?

We have seen numerous worldly and eternal promises which the LORD has detailed in Psalm 91, but the million-dollar question is, who are they for? These promises are not just for everyone who walks as they please. The Psalm itself specifies the conditions of eligibility of enjoying such divine promises.

They are described by three characters: -

Those that know God's name (verse 14)– His nature we cannot fully know, but by his name he has made himself known, and with that we must acquaint ourselves. This means that we must endeavor to know God more than the surface. It is by studying and meditation on the word of God that we get to know him better and better. The more of God we know, the more of His promises are activated in our lives.

Those that set their love upon God (verse 14)– those who rightly know God will love Him. If you love God, you will place your love upon Him as the only adequate object of it. You will let out your love towards God with pleasure and enlargement and will fix your love upon him with a resolution never to remove it to any rival. Jesus explains clearly how we show our love for God: "If ye love me, keep my commandments" (John 14:15). When we obey God's commandments are we find in the scriptures we are practically showing God how much we love Him. As a result, we are eligible for ALL His promises as found in Psalm 91.

Those that call upon God – These are believers who as a result of the personal relationship with the Almighty God through prayer, keep up a constant correspondence with Him, and in every difficult case refer themselves to him. This is quite different from the prayers of a sinner for repentance. This speaks of an intimate conversational relationship. It is not only in the day of trouble that you remember to call upon God. The promises in Psalm 91 are for those who have a habit of always calling upon the LORD – in worship, dedication, adoration, or even in trouble. Truly, no one can call upon someone they haven't been speaking to for help and expect instant deliverance from troubles.

CHAPTER SIX
How Psalm 91 Speaks to Our Health Fears

Psalm 91 is one of the passages in the Bible to which people turn in times of life-threatening diseases, epidemic, pandemic, political, social and financial downturn. Christians, especially, have found the scriptures to be a vital tool (Fagunwa & Fagunwa, 2020). Families and friends quote from this scripture when the pandemic broke out and in other trying times. As we have dug deep into the mysteries of Psalm 91, we find that it is amazing how these are great words of comfort, spoken by God as the protector of those who trust in Him.

This Psalm gave comfort and enhanced recovery for some in sickness and diseases, including Dr. Adaora Okoli-Igonoh, who was infected with the Ebola virus while she was treating the index case in Nigeria in 2014. Adaora, while receiving the best medical treatment said, "Every morning, I began the day with reading and meditating on Psalm 91." (Okoli-Igonoh, 2014).

However, the words which gave Adaora such comfort might seem less efficient or untrue to some who lost loved ones to one health challenge or the other. Suffering disaster is a big question. If God promised protection from evil and satisfaction with long life, why do Christians who have meditated on the scriptures including Psalm 91 suffer, or even die? The reality hits home so hard. Are the words in the Psalm or the entire Bible true? Can we trust the Bible for comfort? The answer of course is yes!

Psalm 91 is replete with assurances that God has marked us for safety. Picture the blood of Passover in the Book of Exodus, when God delivered the children of Israel from the iron fist of Pharaoh. In one night, all the first sons of the Egyptians, including their animals were killed by the death angel. But not one of the children of Israel who put the mark of the blood of Passover as the Lord commanded was hurt. This is what the protection of God is about. Regardless of whatever is happening in the world, like the Israelites, we dwell under the Goshen of God's protection – in the secret place of the Almighty and under the shadow of Yahweh! Glory, Hallelujah!

Even if you have been battling an infection or health issue for long, like the woman with the issue of blood, you will receive your healing as a promise of God in Psalm 91. What is reassuring the most is that God's promises here are even preventive and not just curative. God doesn't even want us to have such sicknesses in the first place. This is what we enjoy when we dwell under His shadow.

However, when we face life-threatening circumstances, such as a pandemic, we can be sure that God will deliver us, whether in life or death. An example is when Satan quoted Psalm 91:11-12 at the time of Jesus' temptation in the wilderness as we rightly observed in the earlier chapters. Satan challenged Jesus to throw himself from the top of a hill, trying to convince Jesus that he will get divine deliverance according to the Psalm. Jesus didn't fall for the temptation because He knew that the promise of Psalm 91 had to be fulfilled in His life through His suffering and death on the cross of Calvary. Psalm 91 was not Jesus' excuse for avoiding the cross; rather that scripture was His reason for going to the cross.

Psalm 91 emphasizes God's protection for those who know Him personally. But God never promised in the New Testament that we will escape sickness, suffering, or even death. Rather, we are promised God's grace and strength to face whatever comes our way (Luke 21:16-18). Paul demonstrated this in his own life. During his first imprisonment, he anticipated "deliverance" from prison (Philippians 1:18-21). However, when he wrote his second letter to Timothy, he knew he was facing potentially deadly treatment at the hands of the evil Roman emperor. At that time, he anticipated "ultimate deliverance" to be with Christ and looked forward to receiving "the crown of righteousness" (2 Tim 4:6-8).

The last 2 verses of Psalm 91 summaries the aim for God's protection – to save us eternally. God has made provision for the greatest rescue and honour (Fagunwa & Fagunwa, 2020). There remains a sure guarantee to satisfy us with everlasting life and show us His salvation. While there are many testimonies of recitation and meditation on Psalm 91 and perhaps recovering from sickness, the Psalm applies to ultimate recovery: salvation.

When we face life-threatening situations, we can be rest assured that for those who dwell under the shadow of the Almighty God, there will be deliverance and recovery whether in life or death. The comfort in Psalm 91 is not a long, trouble-free, pandemic-free life on this present earth, but assurance that those who receive the lordship of Christ will escape the wrath of God which transcends our present experience.

With that said, if all prayers for healing were answered in this life, most Christians would never die. God has a better plan. The message of Psalm 91 could be summed up in the famous saying of

George Whitefield: "We are immortal until our work on earth is done." Or listen to how Pastor Spurgeon captures it:

It is impossible that any ill should happen to the man who is beloved of the Lord; the most crushing calamities can only shorten his journey and hasten him to his reward. Ill to him is no ill, but only good in a mysterious form. Losses enrich him, sickness is his medicine, reproach is his honour, death is his gain. No evil in the strict sense of the word can happen to him, for everything is overruled for good (Spurgeon, Treasury of David, 2016).

Evil and harm cannot separate God's children from Him and that includes pandemics, like the coronavirus, natural disasters, and wicked people among other things. God's children are hidden with Him and their soul is safe with Him for all eternity. We are not guaranteed a pain-free or illness-free life, which is clear in Scripture from the Old
Testament to the New Testament. We read in

Scripture that it is often through strife and struggle that the believer grows spiritually with God and is an encouragement to others (Joseph, Jonah, Abraham, Moses, Esther, Paul, John, and so many others.).

Many of us are obsessed right now by the uncertainty and constantly changing news surrounding the challenges and downturns we experience on the daily, but Psalm 91 assures us that we can't fear what may or may not happen to us. God asks us to trust Him through all situations, and Paul tells us God's grace is sufficient, whether that grace leads to healing or homecoming. Our focus should not be on fear and uncertainty, but the Refuge that our God is present in all circumstances of disease and trouble. We are called to hope and trust in God no matter what is happening in our world. God can be trusted during this period; He is sovereign over the world and your individual life.

CHAPTER SEVEN
How to Activate the Power of Psalm 91 in Your Life Today

> *This book of the law shall not depart out of thy mouth; but thou shalt meditate therein day and night, that thou mayest observe to do according to all that is written therein: for then thou shalt make thy way prosperous, and then thou shalt have good success.*

Joshua 1:8

Our God is a loving God. As you go through God's word, the more you realize that God loves us so much. He does not want anybody to perish. God's wish is to protect us from all kinds of harm as we have found in Psalm 91. His greatest desire is for us to live a fulfilled, protected, and enjoyable life. Unfortunately, God's protective promises are conditional. How can we activate the power of Psalm 91 in our daily lives? How can we live it as a reality 24/7? One powerful way of activating it is by praying it. The second is to meditate on it always.

According to Romance 8:26, the Bible states:

> *Likewise the Spirit also helpeth our infirmities: for we know not what we should pray for as we ought: but the Spirit itself maketh intercession for us with groanings which cannot be uttered.*

The Holy Spirit helps us in our weaknesses. For example, we don't know what God wants us to pray for. But the Holy Spirit prays for us with groanings that cannot be expressed in words.

We really do not know how to pray. This is why we have been given the Holy Spirit. When we remain in God's secret place the Holy Spirit tells us what and how to pray. When we pray the prayer of protection using psalm 91, The Holy Spirit actually helps us and guides us on the words to use. We can hear from the Holy Spirit what to do whenever there is a problem.

Psalm 91 is a prayer for every Christian today. However, to have the psalm 91 testimony and enjoy supernatural protection we need to dwell in the place of prayer. Make it a habit to pray Psalm 91 every day in your family– when you are going to work, school, traveling, etc. When you do so fear disappears. You have absolute trust in God's protection of you and your family no matter what happens.

Another important key to activating Psalm 91 is meditation. You have to create time to meditate on God's Word. The key scripture in Joshua 1:8 shows us the formula for success – meditation and confession of God's Word. When you meditate on Psalm 91 long enough, you walk in the glorious victory of God's redemptive power of protection against all forms of evil. Do not allow fear to overtake you even when you come face to face with troubles.

Our indefatigable God cannot fail us. He is always faithful to fulfill His promises in our lives. All you need to do is position yourself to connect to His neverending protective shadow. Let's conclude with this special Psalm 91 personalized prayer from Heather Riggleman:

Psalm 91 Prayer

Whoever dwells in the shelter of the Most High will rest in the shadow of the Almighty. I will say of the Lord, "He is my refuge and my fortress, my God, in whom I trust." Surely, he will save you from the fowler's snare and from the deadly pestilence He will cover you with his feathers, and under his wings you will find refuge; his faithfulness will be your shield and rampart.

You will not fear the terror of night, nor the arrow that flies by day, nor the pestilence that stalks in the darkness, nor the plague that destroys at midday. A thousand may fall at your side, ten thousand at your right hand, but it will not come near you. You will only observe with your eyes and see the punishment of the wicked.

If you say, "The Lord is my refuge," and you make the Most High your dwelling, no harm will overtake you, no disaster will come near your tent. For he will command his angels concerning you to guard you in all your ways; they will lift you up in their hands so that you will not strike your foot against a stone. You will tread on the lion and the cobra; you will trample the great lion and the serpent.

"Because he loves me," says the Lord, "I will rescue him; I will protect him, for he acknowledges my name. He will call on me, and I will answer him; I will be with him in trouble, I will deliver him and honor him. With long life, I will satisfy him and show him my salvation." (Riggleman, 2020)

BIBLIOGRAPHY

Britannica, T. E. (1998, July 20). *Elohim*. Retrieved from Encyclopedia Britannica: https://www.britannica.com/topic/Elohim

Deffinbaugh, B. (2004, July 04). *God the Protector (Psalm 91)*. Retrieved May 20, 2021, from Bible.org: https://bible.org/seriespage/god-protectorpsalm-91

Della, V. G. (1944). El 'Elyon in Genesis 14:18-20. *Journal of Biblical Literature, 63*(1), 1-9. doi:10.2307/3262503

Fagunwa, A., & Fagunwa, O. E. (2020, October). Pandemic, Pandemonium, and Psalm 91: In Search of Ultimate Protection and Deliverance. *Christ J Glob Health, 7*(4), 1-2.

doi:https://doi.org/10.15566/cjgh.v7i4.461

Havergal, F. R. (1881). *Open Treasures*. J. J. Little & Co: New York.

Kidner, D. (1975). *Psalms 73-150 (Tyndale Commentaries Series)*. Westmont, Illinois: InterVarsity Press.

Martin, J. (2019, September 01). *7 Meanings of Yahweh and Why It's Such an Important Name for God*. Retrieved from Bible Study Tools: https://www.biblestudytools.com/biblestudy/topical-studies/why-it-matters-that-godis-yahweh.html

Matt, D. C. (2004). *The Zohar*. Palo Alto, California: Stanford University Press.

Morgan, G. C. (1978). *Notes on the Psalms*. Michigan: Revell.

Morrison, C. (2017, May 25). *Psalm 91: Dwelling On High*. Retrieved from Rav Kook Torah: http://www.ravkooktorah.org/PSALM-91.htm

Okoli-Igonoh, A. (2014). From the Valley of the

Shadow of Death – Surviving the Dreaded Ebola Disease. *Christ J Global Health*, 1(2), 81-82. doi: https://doi.org/10.15566/cjgh.v1i2.44

Riggleman, H. (2020, April 07). *Why Is Psalm 91 Important During* COVID-19? Retrieved from Christianity.com: https://www.christianity.com/wiki/bible/whyis -psalm-91-important-during-covid-19.html

Sproul, R. C. (2020, June 01). *The Meaning of "El Shaddai"*. Retrieved from Ligonier Ministries : https://www.ligonier.org/blog/meaning- elshaddai/

Spurgeon, C. H. (2011). *Commentary on Psalms 91*. Retrieved from Spurgeon's Verse Expositions of the Bible: https://www.studylight.org/commentaries/eng / spe/psalms-91.html.

Spurgeon, C. H. (2016). *Treasury of David*. Bible Study Steps.

VanderKam, J. (2005). VanderKam, James (July 10, 2005). The Meaning of the Dead Sea Scrolls: Their

Significance for Understanding the Bible, Judaism, Jesus, and Christianity. Bloomsbury Academic.

London: Bloomsbury Academic. Retrieved June 01, 2021, from https://www.google.com/books/edition/The_M eaning_of_the_Dead_Sea_Scrolls/SBMXnB4CR p UC?hl=en&gbpv=0